SLEEPWALK COLLECTIVE X CHRISTOPHER BRETT BAILEY

PSYCHODRAMA

Salamander Street

PLAYS

First published in 2022 by Salamander Street Ltd.
(info@salamanderstreet.com)

Psychodrama © Sleepwalk Collective x Christopher Brett Bailey, 2022

ISBN: 9781914228643

Cover photo by @ladalianegra

10 9 8 7 6 5 4 3 2 1

'I think of a child's mind as a blank book'

Walt Disney

Psychodrama is a show about shows and a story about stories, a half-baked over-blown fairytale which both diligently conforms to and cheerfully betrays storytelling convention. We hope it both succeeds and fails to offer '*a good story, told well*', the narrative cut-up and janky, attempting to escape what's expected of it. It's also a show which – on both its deepest and most superficial levels – is about our own personal relationships with storytelling and about what stories actually are and what they're doing to us, as tellers and listeners and viewers, right now in the early 21st century but also, especially, when we were children. All of which is a roundabout way of saying that *Psychodrama* is fundamentally a show about *television*, the primary storytelling medium of our childhoods plus the primordial model and testing ground for the way in which we now receive and experience most of the world: through a screen.

While this work is created for theatres, it's also something that you the audience are very much *plugged into*, in both a literal sense – text and music are delivered through wireless headphones, our voices forced into your ears, close, disorientating, invasive – and also more metaphorically, the stage here simultaneously a screen-like glow to bathe in and a broadcast you'll be receiving whether you like it or not. Pictures are projected into your head via words, noises, and the crude gestures and gyrations of our onstage anti-heroes. The story takes place, explicitly, within the "landscape of the imagination", and it's pretty cavalier in its treatment of what it finds in there. Like any good head trip or Freudian case study it's mostly sex and violence, but it's a sex and violence that's fundamentally *cartoony*… and literally so… this project emerged out of a joint-fascination with the classic cartoons of the mid-20th century, a number of whose stars will be making cameos pretty soon. We've wondered what happens if we take those stories and the world they describe seriously, what might that do to us and our brains? We've contemplated what would it *actually feel like* to get crushed by an anvil, to have your eyes literally pop out of your heads. And we've realised these cartoons are primal *ur-narratives* – we know their language and grammar well enough that we can see what's about to happen right before it happens – and also, crucially, *anti-narratives*, recursive and looping and consequence-free, always resetting at the beginning of each new episode, and about as shallow as you can make a thing before the substance completely evaporates off. These cartoons appeal to our basest desires – the entertainment equivalent of fast food maybe, and potentially just as unhealthy – but they also have the potential to be anarchic, imaginative, subversive, profound. Whatever they are, we're more or less stuck with them now, these stories and their resident demons are as much a part of us as our own memories.

Psychodrama is a collaborative project in a fairly absolute sense, and the writing has ended up split more or less 50/50 but all mixed up together, authorship shifting back and forth within individual paragraphs and even individual lines. This text arrived – in rehearsal rooms in Madrid and London, and in online docs written together during periods of lockdown in the pandemic-y spring of 2020 – through a long, long process of writing on top of and around each other, and of finishing each other's sentences. Perhaps more than anything else the show has been an excuse to imitate, parody, cartoon-ify and caricature each other's voices. To play with each other's toys. To write further away from ourselves. To hide ourselves inside of a kinda hybrid chimerical voice. To play artistic dress-up.

It was also written as a kind of love letter to each other and to each other's work, to two shows in particular – Chris' *THIS IS HOW WE DIE* and Sleepwalk's *Amusements* – to which it constitutes an informal sequel. In this sense it's a nostalgia trip, a deep-dive down a memory hole, explored and experienced from multiple perspectives – on the one hand, we've each gotten to play around inside the alien form and language and landscape of a show we've loved but have only ever seen from the outside; on the other hand, we've felt allowed to revisit ideas and narratives from our own earlier work, reimagining shows created by our younger selves.

So it's a shared universe! A whole new franchise! A crossover event! A cash grab! And you're in here as well, dear audience. The imagination that this story races through is yours...

We hope you enjoy the ride.

SLEEPWALK COLLECTIVE X CHRISTOPHER BRETT BAILEY

PSYCHODRAMA

Written by Christopher Brett Bailey
and Sammy Metcalfe, with iara Solano Arana

Between 2018 and 2021

Czech translations by Nhung Dang

Psychodrama was made with Beckie Darlington,
Katie Du'Mont, Nhung Dang, and Paola de Diego

We are all sat together, all waiting, each of us
wearing a pair of headphones, which renders us
both together and alone. The lights go down
and then the lights come back up again.
HE sits in front of us. Things now unfold
more or less as described.

HE   Allow yourself to feel at home
Permit yourself that luxury
Put your feet up why not
Not literally, of course
They don't let you put your feet up at the theatre
But you know…
…what I mean
Imagine yourself putting your feet up
Picture yourself at ease
Breath deeply and slowly

Notice that you are breathing deeply and slowly

Before we begin, we have to get ourselves…
…calibrated
You can think of this like it's a kind of foreplay
       if that makes it easier
Or you can think of it like it's something else
Rest assured that this is a routine procedure
We do it every night
In this sense you are like every other audience
       that has come before you
But don't think that means that we can't see you
       from up here
Don't think that means that we can't see you all
       as individuals
Each one of you different and unique
Allow yourselves to feel seen
Allow yourselves to feel appreciated here tonight
Because you are
This is my voice in your left ear
This is my voice in your right ear

This is my voice now asking you to imagine
     a sphere

The sphere is red

Neither dark red nor light red

Just red

Normal red

A normal sphere

Hold the red sphere in your mind's eye

It's important for our purposes
     that you can picture that clearly

Now slowly rotate the sphere

And on the other side of the sphere
     there is a tiny door

And the door opens

And on the other side of the door
     there is a bright white light

And all together we step through the door
     and into the light

And now we are all thinking exactly the same thing
At exactly the same time
And now we're ready to begin

SHE enters with two shots of tequila.

I am sitting behind a table
The table holds objects of indeterminate use
This much you can see
And because you can see it you know it is real
And because you can see it,
	it does not need to be imagined

SHE downs both shots of tequila.

This procedure is considered "safe"
None of what follows is supposed to be difficult
None of what follows is designed to hurt
If anything it's going to hurt us
More than it hurts you
You can think of it like it's television
The sounds and pictures will come
One after another
And they will ask nothing of you
	other than that you feel entertained
Think of this like it's television
And who doesn't love television

Who doesn't love a good story
Told well
Who the fuck doesn't love a good story

*They sit with their heads inside
two TV sets, like children
playing 'TV Presenter'.*

SHE Keep your legs crossed
                 and forget about the real world
         Keep telling yourself:
                 'this is only a show,
                 this is only a show,
                 this is only a show,
                 this is only…'

HE   Keep your mouth closed and your nostrils open
         Keep telling yourself:
                 'I am lost in the static between stations,
                 I am lost in the static between stations,
                 I am lost…'

SHE This transmission happens at a set speed
         Do not attempt to adjust your set

HE   If you want to find us this is who we are:
         Those pesky kids
         Without whom you would've gotten away with it

SHE Dead-eyed teens thrown-up out of the dread
                 hangover of the 1960s
         The summer of love fallen deep
                 into a spooked-out winter
         All dead trees and grey rain

HE   Wastoid toon-hunters chasing nightmares
                 in a psychedelic van
         Legs wheeling underneath us like windmills
         So stoned we think the dog's talking
         Pulling the masks off one after another
         To reveal the sweaty pink faces underneath

SHE The old guy from the funfair
         The old woman from the house on the hill
         Raincoat perverts and corrupt cops
                 and drowned girls
         Butchered starlets

Prepubescent Pageant girls
            and homecoming queens
Illicit children locked in the basement as sex slaves
Young lovers making out in parked cars
Ghosts and ghouls from haunted houses
Pulling the masks off one by one
Until we get down to the fucking skull

HE   If you want to find us this is where we are:
In every tribe, commune, dormitory,
farmhouse, barracks and townhouse
Where kids are making love, smoking dope
            and loading guns

SHE   Some we kill for money
Some we kill for fun
Some we kill just to watch the ink splatter
            across the empty page

HE   Turning your childhood heroes into ghosts

SHE   Now watch our eyes glaze over
As we fall into one of our episodes...

Light. Smoke. The sound of wind.

HE   Morning finds the desert stretched out
        in front of us like a yellow ocean
    And a road cutting forever through it
    Straight as an arrow or a scalpel cut
    Just one long straight road across
        this whole goddamn state

SHE   The road is lined with cacti
        and bleached animal bones
    We speed past a solitary gas station

HE   '…I feel odd, I feel weird, I'm getting déjà vu…'

SHE   And I push the accelerator and I say
    'Shh, darling, déjà vu is rarely terminal'
    And we are on it now
    On the road
    And he is reading aloud from the tourist guide
    Which is telling us that the top speed
        of your average Greater Roadrunner
        is 32 kilometres per hour…

HE   …but then, this ain't no average bird…

SHE   …so we've got the pedal floored
    And the van judders and roars
    A blue-green streak
    Blurring past coyotes
    Coyotes setting traps and building rockets

HE   Coyotes painting tunnels onto mountains

SHE Coyotes leading lines of lost children
         towards a sun-blitzed horizon
         Towards a border fence like a crooked row of teeth
         A border fence that is the end of Amerika
         in more ways than one
         And still we blur onwards
         Faster and faster

HE Towards a pin-prick vanishing point
         that will one day swallow us all

SHE Towards the future

HE Until out of that future there fades a distant figure
         Moving impossibly fast but we are somehow faster

SHE And as we get closer
         The figure gradually materialises into the shape
         of a running bird
         So much larger than the photo in the guidebook
         Colours brighter and more garish
         That's how we know it's him

HE It's definitely him
         And as we get closer she screams:

                              SHE pulls out a tiny megaphone.

SHE He is so much larger than he looks on TV!!!!

HE The bird runs with legs windmilling
         Tornado-ing,
         Hurricaning,
         beneath him,
         Eyes deadpan and ashen
         Beak opening and closing
         Although whatever sound it's making –
         whatever he is trying to say

– is buried under the growling grunting
          piston pumping of our engine
Oblivious, he runs on
Running god knows where
Thinking god knows what

SHE   (…although this last question will be answered
          real soon if you just stay tuned…)

HE   And now I'm leaning out the window
          and I can smell the tyres melting
And my eyes are getting pushed back
          into their sockets
And forced backwards into my brain
And my hands grip the baseball bat
And as we hit terminal velocity –
or so it seems to me
– and as the bird rushes straight towards us
I swing

SHE   And there is
Just
The
Most
Extraordinary
Sound
(A sonic boom of shattering bone
          and splintering wood and rushing air
          like a church imploding!)

HE   And she stamps her foot deep into the floor
Slamming on the brakes
So hard her foot goes through the bottom of the car
And her high heel penetrates the blacktop,
          sparks start flying

SHE   And we screech to a sudden stop

HE   So sudden in fact that I'm thrown
           straight out the window
And carried by that outrageous momentum
I am spread like strawberry jam across 100 metres
           of road in front of us
But I'm still in good spirits
I'm still in good spirits of course
Because The Job is already halfway done

SHE   Looking back another 100 metres behind us
           we see the bird
Collapsed like an umbrella at the side of the road

HE   We saunter up
All casual like
And when we get close enough
I say 'hit record on the thing'
She says 'what thing?'
I say 'the gizmo'
She says 'which gizmo?'
I say 'the thing-a-me-bob'
She says 'there are two thing-a-me-bobs here,
           which one do you mean?'
I say 'fuck, are you dumb or do you just play dumb
           so you don't have to do anything?'

SHE   I push the record button on the thing-a-me-bob
Because we want a permanent record of this one
To capture his last words,
           to savour them for all time,
To re-enact them later, to relive this moment again
           and again and again and again

A movie screen flickers into life.

IT *Nahrává se…*
Nahrává se…

Pokusím se vám to nyní vysvětlit
Pokusím se vám to vysvětlit, přestože tomu stejně
nebudete, nedokážete a ani nemůžete
porozumět
Pokusím se vám to vysvětlit následovně:
Existuje rychlost, při níž všechny barvy
krvácí doběla
Existuje rychlost, při níž všechny cesty krvácí
nahoru směrem k nebi
Existuje rychlost, při níž vás předstihnou všechny
vaše myšlenky a celá vaše mysl, a vůbec
všechny možnosti vašeho přemýšlení,
smýšlení a uvažování
Můj bože, tohle – tohle – byste měli vidět
Pokud jste někdy jedinkrát v životě cítili vítr
ve vlasech
Pokud jste někdy jedinkrát v životě dostali
při zrychlení smyk a zalapali těžce
po dechu
Kdybych tak mohla přeběhnout přes celou tuhle
poušť a přes celou Ameriku
Kdybych tak mohla proběhnout přes tenhle žlutý
písek a přes tu nekonečnou silnici, která
se ve smyčce dokola opakuje a zas a znova
se vrací
Jako Möbiova páska, jako had se kroutí 24 snímků
za vteřinu a snaží se marně dosáhnout
horizontu
Kdybych tak mohla předběhnout i kojot–

I am going to try to explain this to you
I am going to try although you will not, and cannot, understand
I am going to explain it like this:
There is a speed at which all colours bleed into white
There is a speed at which the road bleeds into the sky
There is a speed at which you outrun your thoughts and all thinking
and all possibility of thinking
My god you should see it

> If you have ever felt the wind in your hair
> If you have ever felt the jolt of acceleration and gasped
> If I could outrun this desert and all Amerika
> If I could outrun this yellow sand and endless road looping like a Möbius strip
> Snaked across 24 frames per second and towards an unreachable horizon
> If I could outrun the Coyot-

The screen cuts suddenly to black.

HE   And with that… the bird's beak falls shut at last
And the eyes blacken
And The Job is done
We photograph the corpse for proof
For payment
Some we kill for money, some we kill for food
Some we kill just to see the ink splatter
      across the empty page

SHE   That night
Under a desert sky basted with stars
We roast our prize over an open fire
By the morning there will be nothing left
Except a pile of bones amongst other bones

HE   We read in the paper a week or so later
That the coyote wept
Upon hearing the news
And said to the reporters:
      'What am I gonna do with my life now?
      Chasing that fuckin' bird was the whole
      point of my existence. I'm like Sisyphus
      now, without a rock.'

A tinny theme tune plays.
HE and SHE remove their TV sets.
The lights shift. The movie screen returns.

IT   *Dobrá, toto je sezení 21 B*
          Naposledy jste mi, Chrisi, povídal o svém dětství
          Co kdybychom se k tomu nyní vrátili a vy byste mi
                  o svém dětství pověděl více?

Ok, this is session 21B

Last time, Chris, you were telling me about your childhood

How about we pick up from where we left off?

HE   In this memory I am six years old
          It's late afternoon
          My parents are away again
          And so I sit in the same TV wash I always sit in
          And in front of me I see the same crudely drawn
                  figures as I see every day
          The same anthropomorphic animals beating
                  the same cartoon shit out of each other
          Except this time I realise that when I close my eyes
                  they're still there
          The grinning shapes are inside me now
          Inside my head
          Seeing through my eyes, reading my thoughts,
                  telling me what to do
          And I know in this moment that there is something
                  horribly wrong

IT   *Pokračujte…*

Go on…

HE   My imagination is no longer my own
          It has been somehow occupied
          Colonised
          That what was once limitless possibility
          An inner landscape without edges or borders
                  or control
          Now lives under the heavy boot of a cartoon rabbit
                  and a cartoon mouse
          That I will forever see the world as if through
                  a glowing screen

That I was meant to have been somebody else
Somebody better
We all were

IT   *A iaro, jak vy se ohledně toho cítíte?*

                                    And iara, how does that make you feel?

SHE I see it like this:
In the landscape of the imagination
        it is always kill or be killed
If we are to be free
Truly free
We must hunt down these mice and rabbits
These grinning spectres
And subject them to the most awful violence
            imaginable
Like this is the only kind of imagination
        that is truly left to us
To imagine the worst until we transcend ourselves
To push deeper into the nightmare
Until we can call it our own
And through this violence
        we will wash our brains clean

IT   *Řekněte mi o tom, prosím, více*

                                              Tell me more

SHE No

IT   *Chrisi, co tím iara asi myslí, když říká*
        'push deeper into the nightmare'?

                Chris, what do you think she means by 'push deeper into the nightmare'?

HE   She means that every night
Armed to the teeth
We tune the television to static
And slip down the crack between stations

Where we find ourselves in a familiar landscape
Of exploding thought-bubbles
        and rubberised anatomy
Of exaggerated sound effects
        and overly-illustrative music
And a long, long road
        stretching towards a distant horizon
Towards an ending

SHE Let's hope the road goes on forever
Because what could possibly be waiting for us
        once this war is over?
Cruel inertia
'Cause peacetime is deathtime for weapons
Us weapons need conflict
Like a bullet needs a target
Like teeth need meat
And need
Need is deeper
Than love
So, let's you and me learn to love each other
        inside this need
Inside this fight
Inside this war

HE Let's dance to the sizzling thwack
        of a hot metal tyre iron to the face
To the wire jaws of a mousetrap grinning
        and snapping shut
To the blackened thumbnail falling off the finger
To the tweeting of canaries round a skull
        with throbbing Xs for eyes
To the flightpath of ghosts as they exit corpses
        and waft towards heaven
To the skinned body floating facedown in a river
To the body parts of anonymous women piling up
        in dumpsters around the world
To the young girl who had her arms cut off and got
        kicked out of the back of a moving van,

falling to her almost death at the bottom
of a ravine on the outskirts of town
To the once pretty face burned by acid
To the knife entering a pregnant belly
Because all these deaths are temporary
So long as the war keeps raging

SHE Lucky for us
Our mission will never be complete

IT *A kde si myslíte, že jste teď?*

And where do you think you are right now?

SHE In a diner

IT *Zavřete oči a popište mi to*

Close your eyes and describe it for me

SHE I see… plastic tables
Black and white tiles
A jukebox in the corner
A waitress in a polkadot dress

IT *Výborně*
A nyní mě tam vemte

Good
Now take me there

Ambient diner sounds fade in,
muted voices and clinking cutlery, etc…

HE So… we went out for a milkshake
To celebrate
Sat in a corner booth
Red vinyl seats
A greasy fry cook with a mentholated cigarette
Dangling from her lips
A waitress rollerskates over to our table:
> 'We have… Coca Cola, Dr Pepper, Sprite,
> 7up, Mountain Dew, Cream Soda, Root
> Beer, Grape Crush, Orange Crush, Cherry
> Coke, Vanilla Coke, Pepsi Cola, Gatorade,
> Powerade, Lemonade, Diet Dr Pepper,
> Diet Coca Cola, Diet Caffeine Free Coca
> Cola, Diet Sprite, Diet Mountain Dew,
> Caffeine Free Mountain Dew, Mountain
> Dew Code Red, Diet Cherry Coke, Diet
> Cherry Vanilla Dr Pepper, Diet Pepsi,
> Pepsi Max and Coke…with…Lime'

I say, 'We'll have our usual…
two… fucking… milkshakes'

HE and SHE slurp their milkshakes.

SHE I look at him across the table
His heart is beating visibly in his chest
His eyes turn into telescopes
And come across the table towards me
Drinking in my contours and curves
And I say 'what the fuck are you up to?'

HE I flutter my eyelashes like the wings of a dove
And I say 'I'm overflowing with emotion'
And I…
And I…
And I suggest we go somewhere we can be alone
And she says:

SHE 'Why don't we just make whoopee right here?'

Sax-heavy 'erotic' disco music starts to play.

SHE My god
The things you do to me
Watch me beating my fists on the table
Watch my eyeballs grow plate-sized and pop out
      of my head
Watch my mouth drop open and my tongue roll out
      along the floor
I'm sweating
I can hardly control myself
Watch my heart-shaped heart beating out
      of my chest
Beating through my clothes
Watch the heart-shaped hearts spinning in my eyes
This is what you do to me
This is you reducing me to an animal
Frothing at the mouth and chomping at the bit
Whistling and howling

HE Watch me pop a boner like a pool cue
Like a battle axe
Like a broad sword
Watch me pop a boner like the cannon
      of a naval gunship
You spread yourself like segments of orange
Like butter on toast
And slide me inside you like
That pole meat rotates around
At the kebab shop
We bounce
Elegantly tumbling over each other
Like slinkies going down spiral staircases
We sweat
Rusting the springs of the bench in our booth
And we rot the wood of the table

Your eyes loll back into your head
Your jaw clenches
Your nipples harden
Your clitoris vibrates like a bumblebee
Is trapped beneath your flesh
I press my thumb against it
Try to squash the bumblebee
And you flood the booth
With gelatinous white excretions
Your nipples lactate
Snot pours from your nose
Your coño sprays
Liquid serotonin
And auburn chunks of menstrual blood
Hurtle from your crotch
Like rocks from a slingshot
I smear them over my naked form
And howl at the ceiling fan
And the peeling wallpaper
And the picture of James Dean on the wall
And the black and white tiles and the jukebox
And the waitress who is rollerskating
Through puddles of our come and our blood
And secretly touching herself under her apron
Big tiddies Gainax-bouncing along with the music
We analyse the splatter on the walls
     like an inkblot test
You see a marijuana leaf
I see a renaissance portrait of myself
I always see a renaissance portrait of myself

SHE We roll around in the ick and the spray
And we do it again
In a position that would make
     a wheelbarrow blush
I slide up and down him like a firehouse pole
He eats me like cantaloupe or watermelon
Swallowing my moisture and spitting out my seeds
I quake

And our table collapses
So I peg him with each of the four table legs
Sliding the wood into his rectum
His spine stiffens
And he has a butt-gasm
His mouth opens
And out sprays a million wood splinters

HE   I get down on all fours and I worship her feet
I tongue her toes and nibble her nails
And bite off her bunions
I peel dead skin off her heel
And I wear it like a condom
As I fuck the gap between her big toe
        and her index toe

SHE   And before long my foot is wearing a slipper
Made of su leche
Feet aren't really my thing
But relationships are about compromise
It's give and it's take
So I ask him to take me for the big finish
He doesn't like it but he'll do it for me
Because he loves me
I adopt the slave position
And I spread my dirt peach
He tongues my anal lips
He puckers up and inhales
He sucks so hard my intestines unspool
And hurtle out of my asshole
At a velocity that makes me
Briefly die
A little death
And I go to heaven

HE   The fry cook runs in with a bucket and mop
I sprout angel wings and float up from the table
And see that YOU are there in the diner

Spurting into an empty milkshake glass
Memorising all these details for later
So when you are humping
In your loveless relationship
You can picture the two of us instead
I flap my angel wings
And float to heaven
Where we're going to fuck everyone who has ever lived:
…Your great-great grandmother, Gandhi,
     Joan of Arc, Napoleon, J. Robert
     Oppenheimer, Henry Kissinger, Henry
     Miller, Corey Haim, the guy who stuck the
     spear in Jesus *(as in Christ)*, Maya
     Angelou, Walt Disney, Tex Avery, J. Stuart
     Blackton, Henry Darger, Babe Ruth, Sei
     Shōnagon, The Fleischer Brothers, E.C.
     Segar, Clara Bow, Helen Kane, Jackie
     Gleason, Arthur Janov, R.D. Laing, Philip
     Seymour Hoffman, Mark Antony,
     Jonbenét Ramsey, Frida Kahlo, Anaïs
     Nin, Sharon Tate, Jayne Mansfield,
     Michael Jackson, Riley Gale, Glenn
     Branca, Genghis Khan, And YOU…
When YOU arrive in heaven
Having slipped off this mortal coil
We will be waiting to greet you
Me with my cowboy boots and
     armoured breast-plate
Naked where it counts, with a hardon in one hand
And a harp in the other
She'll be in her chainmail stockings
Doing…whatever she thinks she's doing right now
Whatever *that* is, whatever it's supposed to be,
          but more so
Cranked to eleven
Both of us will be waiting for you
     and so will all our goons
Our squad
Our gang

Because as you know and I know and we all know
        all too well
Everyone and everything we kill in this life
Will be our slave in the afterlife
A goofy dog and a duck in half a sailor suit
Blue cats and brown mice
        and yellow tweeting birds
A st-st-st-stuttering p-p-p-pig in a b-b-b-bow tie
We'll all be waiting for *You* at the pearly gates
Oiled up, greased up, lubed up and ready to go
Just imagine that
Picture that
Picture
Imagine
Picture
Imagine
My god…

SHE An important principle of psychodrama
Of drama therapy
Is that just because something is imaginary
Just because it's 'pretend'
That doesn't mean it isn't actually happening
Something is always happening
Even if we would prefer that it wasn't
I describe a long road winding through a desert
I describe it perfectly and there it is
You can see it
I describe myself putting my hands
        around his throat
And squeezing
Until he spasms
And turns purple
And tweeting birds circle his head
And there we are
Here we are
Inside you
Behind your eyes
Doing it

I describe for you a car crash
An airline disaster
A falling bomb with a smouldering pin-up
        painted on the side
I describe for you a kiss
I describe all the things that I would do to you
        personally
If we could have just five minutes alone
At the same time though it is assumed that this
        is still a safe place
Where we can test things safely on one another
Before we try them out in our own homes
And perhaps by rehearsing the worst
We will be ready when the time comes
And perhaps by pretending to be someone else
We can find out who we really are

A tinny theme tune plays.
A bomb goes off.
Blackout.

EPISODE 99
BLOW ME DOWN

Nautical sounds and a familiar theme tune
play off an old vinyl record. Light again,
and more smoke. HE wears an un-inflated
inflatable arm, flaccid like a used condom.
SHE blows into it. The arm inflates.

HE   I am not a violent man
Not by nature
I wouldn't hurt a fly
I know how to be gentle with these hands
And that is how I would prefer these hands to be
That is how I would prefer things to stay
Between you and me
But I understand that there is sometimes work
      to be done
That one must roll up one's sleeves
And get one's hands dirty
Because someone has to do it
I am not a violent man
But if you touch her
If you touch one hair on her head
I will…
Inflate you through the urethra
Until you burst
Like a birthday balloon
I will squeeze you like a tube of toothpaste
Like I'm trying to get the last brush-load out of you
I will take a class in Japanese Hibachi cooking
So I can cut you up and fry you
And stand outside Tokyo train station selling you
      to tourists at an inflated price
I will clone you
And sell the clone
As a sex slave
to your father

But I hope it won't come to that
I hope we won't get anywhere *near* that…

    …tonight

But I am
What I am
And I know it
I know who this man is inside of me
        and I have learnt to live with him
And I will eat the spinach if I'm forced to
Squeeze the can and catch the spinach in my mouth
        and eat it
And it will be like opening a door
And letting that other man out
That ass-chinned one-eyed sadist
Who will not and cannot be controlled
I will let him into this body
And into these muscles bulging and clanging
        like bells
I will eat the spinach and then
        you'll really see something

Because after all I am
What I am
What I am
What I am
What I am
What I am
What I am
What I am…

                                        The arm is now fully inflated
                                            and fully erect.

Unless I'm *not* what I am
Unless I'm not *me*
But if *I'm* not me then who is?
And who am *I?*

And if I'm somebody else and somebody else is me
       then why do I look like me?
This sure sounds like my voice but maybe it isn't
'I am what I am' – I say that all the time
But maybe I say it because it isn't true
'I am what I am' – wrong! – There is no stable or
essential 'me', I am an amalgamation of every
book, movie, TV show I've consumed, every song
I've sung, and every lover I've taken. I've never had
a thought that I would consider 'mine', to think
that would be blindly egotistical. Sometimes I'll
think that I've had an original thought or idea…
And then at 2AM I'm watching an old movie on TV
and the protagonist will say 'my' thought.

Obviously I have taken his words, internalised
them, and made them my own. And of course they
weren't 'his words' at all…

'I y'am what I y'am and that's all that I y'am'
'I'm strong to the finish cause I eats me spinach'

The movie screen returns.

IT   *Tohle je nyní sezení 32 K*
       Chtěla bych začít otázkou. Pociťujete, že už
            byste měli zdravé porozumění o tom,
               kým jste?

                        This is now session 32K
      I want to begin by asking if you feel like you have a healthy understanding of
                            who you are right now?

HE   No

IT   *Jak dlouho si myslíte, že jste zde byli?*

                         How long do you think you've been here for?

HE   I don't know

IT   *Vzpomenete si na to, kdy jste naposledy slyšeli jiný*
        hlas než můj?

                        Can you remember the last time you heard a voice other than mine?

HE   No

IT   *A přijde vám to něčím zvláštní?*

                        And doesn't that seem strange to you?

HE   …

IT   *Co si přejete z tohoto všeho odnést?*

                        What are you hoping to get from all this talking?

HE   I don't know
        Understanding, maybe
        Even the worst people need to feel understood
        And we *are* the worst people, we know that

IT   *A cítíte se nyní být chápán?*

                        And do you feel understood now?

HE   Not really

IT   *Pojďme se tedy vrátit zpátky na začátek, k tomu*
        okamžiku, kdy jste se poprvé potkali

                        Let's try going back to the beginning then, to when you first met

BACKSTORY

(or: The *True Crime* industry is built on
the torture and murder of young
women... *Boop-Oop-a-Doop!*)

SHE He found me tied to a traintrack
Or chained to a radiator
Or strapped to a bed in a burnt-out basement
Or bound and gagged in a refrigerator
My prepubescent body had been scrunched up
         and stuffed into the vegetable drawer
Do you want to hear this?
My wrists were bruised, arms broken
Do you want me to go on?
My knickers stained from innocence stolen
My purple lips were bulbous and swollen
Do stop me if you think
    you've heard this one before
You've heard this one before
Stop me

HE I pulled her out, uncut her ties
I threw her over one shoulder
    and I took her outside
And it's then that I recognised her
She looked different back then:
Short, ink-black hair and skin as white as paper
Huge eyes
And a tiny mouth like a raspberry
The moon was sobbing from what had been done
      to her
  That's really all there is to say...

SHE I screamed all the screams I'd held in
    while the southern fried chicken
    had his way with me
An air raid siren tore from my voicebox

HE   I could see tonsils waggling at the back
                    of her throat
     My ears turned to glass and then shattered
     My heart dissolved and inside it was another heart
     A real one
     Not the iconic cartoon heart like an upside down
                   triangle with tits on top
     But the real McCoy

SHE   A genuine human heart
     Beating visibly in his chest
     Ba boom, Ba boom, Ba boom

HE   And then her heart dissolved
     And inside it was a rubik's cube
     I reached into her chest cavity
     Pulled out the rubik's cube
     Shook off the gore
     Scratch that, I licked off the gore
     Scratch that, I let the rain wash away the gore
     And I solved the rubik's cube
     And put it back inside her
     And the skin sealed over
     Like the wound was never there

SHE climbs onto the table.
HE follows her and kneels before her.
HE blows into her crotch.
Her belly slowly inflates.

SHE He gets down on his knees
And I ask him to make a woman of me
His face is completely expressionless
His eyes are empty
Like the eyes of a sheep or of a cow
But he complies
And I ask myself:
Why not him
After all, why not him
He is the man of my dreams
The dreams where I'm falling
The dreams where I'm lost in the woods
All my dreams
Scattered like dead leaves on the ground
Am I dreaming now
My love
My mother told me
About boys like you
With your cracked lips and broken promises
With your nuclear eyes
And something else
Something important
But I wasn't listening closely enough
Hi mum
Look at me now
Look at what you made
Hi Chris
Let's tell ourselves a story and put ourselves in it
Let's pretend
Let's make love
Let's make a baby
Let's 3D-print ourselves a tiny body that is you
          and me both together
The best and worst of us, all squeezed
     into one single person
Let her be beautiful

HE   And just like that
We retcon our lives into a romance
A love story
Something more tender
It's not that the sex and violence are removed
It just that they feel different now
Like we didn't really mean any of it
Like it wasn't such a big part of it all
Like it was an accident, a quirk of the narrative
Soft-focus and slapstick and lighthearted
We rewrite the past so we can write ourselves
          a new future
Because maybe we *can* stop this ride and get off it
Maybe this life *isn't* a chair we're all strapped into
With our eyes pinned open and a signal pulsing
          into our brains
Maybe there is no god, no author hovering over us
          and telling us who we have to be
Perhaps, somewhere, there's an escape route
          that we haven't thought of yet
A new idea, waiting to be born…

Suddenly everything stops.

IT   *Tenhle příběh má jen jeden konec*
A my k němu míříme, ať už chcete nebo ne
          Žádná míra představivosti to teď nemůže
               změnit

This story only has one ending
And we're going there whether you like it or not
No amount of imagining can change that now

Říkejte si sami sobě dokola: 'Tohle je jenom show,
          tohle je jenom show, tohle je jenom show'

Keep telling yourself: 'this is only a show,
this is only a show, this is only a show'

HE and SHE get back inside their TV sets.
The TV sets glow green.

SHE   We jump the fence at the Magic Kingdom
Long shadows stretch across moonlit too-green grass
           and creaking fairground rides
And the pathways are littered
           with fun's sparkled debris
And occasional patches of pink vomit
From when the fun got too much
This is hallowed ground, alright
Preteen dreams cloud the air like thick smoke
And the white castle looms ghostly in the distance
We vault the turnstile
And duck the security guards
And I glance over and his teeth are already bared
Wolf-like
No longer puppyish
And there is something in his eyes
           that is no longer recognisable
It is not anger or zeal
But nor is it any kind of professional steeliness
This one will be personal

HE   We jump the fence at the Magic Kingdom
And run down Main Street USA
On your left is Casey's Corner,
           a 1950's baseball hot dog eatery
On your right, an ice cream parlour
There are signs for Tomorrowland
           and Adventureland
And about a million different gift shops
But we are heading for the castle
Because this here is the big one

So my blood runs thick and cold
And I am breathing deeply and slowly
And I have noticed myself breathing
      deeply and slowly

SHE   We scale the castle wall with a grappling hook
And halfway up
Through a window ringed by plastic bricks
We see them for the first time:
Mr and Mrs Mouse

HE   They have the worn-in ease of an old couple
She's reclining on a gold-threaded couch
And he's over at the stove
Oversized ladle in a white-gloved hand
His lips are moving but the blood roars in our ears
      so we don't hear…

SHE   Then we're through the window
      in one fluid movement
And there is no time for fucking around
      or for thinking
And Mrs Mouse barely has time to register
      her surprise
'we are the devil and we're here to do the devil's
      business' I say and I almost mean it
She squeaks in her helium voice 'please don't kill
      me, I don't want to die', or whatever
I clutch my bump tenderly, and say 'I have to,
      for my baby'
As I take a hammer to the top of her head

HE   Mr Mouse in on the floor now too
And My Only Girl swings around
      and is on the floor with him
And tears are flooding down her face
And with her lips now fully inside one massive ear
      she's screaming:

SHE & HE	You first came to me when I was too young
	to know any better
	Broke in through the television
	like a home invader
	Through the wrong end of the cathode ray
	You came to me as a friend
	And gave me all these things
	pretending they were gifts
	A candysoaked version of love
	A saccharine joy
	Pushed down the ear canal
	Poured in through the eye sockets
	Sticky as ice cream
	Thick as cement
	And now I am full of you
	You are the acid and bile
	caught in my throat
	The hole ripped through my head
	You are the thing that walks my dreams
	every night
	And I want to wake up now

HE	Now I'm straddling his chest
	And my courage is boiling off me like steam
	And my indifference is curling off me like smoke
	And I am sweating
	And I am feeling things
	Despite myself
	Things exploding inside my head
	like light bulbs shattering
	All of these sensations could be clearly catalogued
	and defined
	None of them are in any way sexual
	And now his eyes dart wildly
	As I put my hands around his throat

SHE	On the other side of the room Mrs Mouse
	is bleeding out
	We take a ceremonial sword down off
	the castle wall

And use it to slice off one giant ear
And throw it across the room like an enormous
      black frisbee

HE   When I was a child I spoke as a child
I understood as a child
I thought as a child
But when I became a man
      I put away childish things

It's time to grow up

Mr Mouse is coming round so I straddle him again
And he slowly begins to raise his arms
As if gesturing or waving
At some audience I cannot see
And then I realise:
He's asking me for a hug
Of course he's asking for a hug
His nerves firing in a final impulse
The last transmission from a dying synapse
He reaches for a hug and I sink into it
How could I refuse?
I am not a monster
How many children has he held like this?
I am five years old again
I'm going to throw up

SHE reaches through the TV screen
and aims a gun at the audience.

SHE   'Enough emotion!' I scream 'Enough foreplay!'
His mouse-life is flashing before his eyes
He sees himself first in colour
      and then in black and white
His memory rewinds all the way back
To when he was nothing but the lead
      in his creator's pencil
Fingers twitching in a giant glove
As if to give one final autograph

A gloved arm reaches through one of the TV sets.
HE produces a chainsaw and chops the arm off.

SHE   I snuggle up to the corpse
And tenderly kiss what is left of its face
I dildo myself to oblivion with a severed limb
We carefully rearrange the scene
Placing this hand here, and this hand there
Just right
Until the whole thing looks like an accident
A domestic dispute gone awry
A mistake
A joke that went too far

A tinny theme tune plays.

Ambient diner sounds fade in again,
muted voices and clinking cutlery, etc…

HE   We go out for milkshakes to celebrate
Fry cook
Cigarette
Waitress: 'Ohhh... You two again
                Ya want yer fuckin' usual?'

SHE slurps her milkshake.

HE sits in silence.

SHE   'What's eating you?' I ask
        without really wanting to know

HE   I was just thinking...

SHE   Uh oh...

HE   What if...what if we've had things the wrong way around
since the beginning?
What if the imagination *isn't* limitless possibility,
        what if it's actually kind of...empty?

SHE   Don't make that serious face
It doesn't suit you
Just look at yourself
Look at your hair
Look at *my* hair...

HE   No, really, listen
This time I think I mean what I'm saying...
What if the television was trying to give us
        something we actually *need*
Maybe without television we'd be like...
        frightened little animals,
                with no idea who we are
Maybe we actually *need* a cartoon rabbit
      and a cartoon mouse and a cartoon duck
      in half a sailor suit to show us how to live
To animate us

Otherwise our minds would be just…blank pages

SHE   That's depressing

HE   I mean, try it now
Try to imagine something new
Something you've never seen before
Something original for once
Something that's actually yours
Try to picture…

…and I want to continue but she's long since belched
and left the table, crossed the room, her red shoes
clip-clopping the diner floor. And now she pulls
from the pocket of her pinafore, a coin the size of a
dinner plate. She slides the coin into the jukebox,
mashes a couple of buttons and the world goes all…

The jukebox lights up.
A song plays. SHE dances.
The Jukebox sings in a high pitched
voice, artificial and vulnerable…
like a newborn robot. SHE lip-syncs.

JUKEBOX

my soul aches
my heart breaks
i cry lakes

you coil
like a snake
in the hole that you make
in my heart

you shake
me to my shoes

you gift
me the blues
you gift
me this bruise

you take
and you take
and you take
it all from me

you wake
and you wake
and you wake
up from me

i ache
and i break
and when i don't
i fake
it all for you

a mistake
a mistake
you were my mistake
but you made me

HE   You are a machine for watching
Listening
Consuming
Us
Your responses are automatic
You sit in your seat like a severed limb
Like a baby in the womb
Writhing in response to the show
To the lights
To the sounds
To the touch
Of us
You are not so complicated
You are buttons and levers of flesh
Piping shuttles blood
A primitive sewer system coils
In your belly like a brown snake
And at the place beneath your belly
Where your legs come together
There are hot embers like coals
Or the lit tip of a cigarette

SHE   Getting hotter
Getting brighter
With every drag

HE   I'm going to take my trousers off now
Underneath them are blue jeans
I am going to take my blue jeans off now
My jockey shorts
My boxers
My briefs
I am going to take my condom off now

Okay, it's off

And the condom
Can represent
Whatever
You want it to represent

SHE   The flickering lights represent television
A cathode ray transmission
The cable connected to you
Represents the umbilical
Delivering sounds and stories
Into you
But what if it is a two way street
And it is also
Sucking parts of you out

HE   Each and every one of you
Is a vital cog
In the audience machine
A battery
From which we suck power
And we are tongues and lips
Robots of speech and story

SHE   With story after story
We try to bore you to death
        but you fuckers refuse to die
We take turns inflating ourselves into the man
        and woman we would like to be
Or the man and woman we are expected to be
Pregnant, muscle-bound,
        like this is all our bodies are good for
Like these bodies are what the story demands
Until we arrive at the end of one final escapade
        and there's suddenly a twist
        in the narrative
And we find ourselves stepping together
        into a room

And we find ourselves stood in front of a group
        of strangers
All plugged into some mysterious machine

HE   And I find myself saying:
            'Allow yourself to feel at home
            Permit yourself that luxury
            Put your feet up why not…'

SHE   And as he starts to speak we look closer
And in that crowd of strangers
We see *you*
Sitting in the dark
Eyes open but somehow unseeing
Falling into the trap that the story was setting
        right from the beginning
As trapped now inside the narrative as we are

Hi…
    Hello…
        Open your ears…
            Enough foreplay…
                We're coming in…
                    You can close your eyes now…

Complete and utter blackout.

The whispered voices of SHE and HE
now sound so close it's like they're
tiny and standing right on your earlobe.

HE   Hello you

SHE   It's us

HE   We're right here, on your ear

A knocking sound.

SHE   Can we come in?

HE   You can trust us

SHE   We're nice really, once you get to know us

HE   We really are
Picture a door opening…

The sound of a door opening in your ear
HE and SHE now sound like they're walking
down your ear canal, arriving inside your head.

HE   Wow!

SHE   The opulence!

HE   I've never seen anything so beautiful

SHE   Is this real marble? Is that real gold?

HE   I don't know, seems kind of squishy…

SHE   Don't step on that!

HE   Oops… Well, they probably don't really need it…

SHE   Hey look at all those paintings on the wall!

HE   Do you think it's their exes?

SHE   Kind of…ugly?

HE   Yeah. And wait, over there, is that…

SHE   Yeah, Chris, it's that red sphere you made…
           Looks like it's been in here for years…

HE   Hey! There's a door on this side of it…
           And there are steps going down…
           They go deeper and deeper and deeper inside…

> *The two go down the staircase,*
> *deeper into your head.*
> *You hear the door in the red sphere*
> *closing with a thud behind them…*

HE   Now we're in here you can really show us something
           Picture the last time you had sex
           Hold that scene in your mind's eye,
                 so that we can see it too

SHE   Now show us your first love
           The love of your life
           The one that got away
           Show us…the house where you grew up
           Show us your primal scene

HE   Show us you
           Hurtling backwards through time
           Through work
           School
           Infancy
           Learning to walk
           To crawl
           All the way back into the womb

SHE   Point at yourself in these memories
And say: 'that's me'
And mean it
Then tell us: is your performance consistent
How much of your life did you rehearse beforehand
       in a bathroom mirror

HE   And is your performance good enough
Or have you tweaked your memories
And left some of them on the cutting room floor
Show us the parts that you edit out

SHE   Tell me:
What are the stories
That you tell yourself
About yourself
And are they believable
Are they believable enough
What stories do you tell yourself
       in order to sleep at night
Are they fully your own
Or did you borrow them from somewhere else
Someone else's movie
The sudden twist
The broken heart
The heartwarming lesson

HE   And while the real world burns around
       the edges of your story
Trying to get in
You might ask yourself:
Who's narrating this anyway?
Who are all the voices inside your head?
And how did they get there?

SHE   And if you can't tell exactly where you end
       and all these other voices begin
That can perhaps be forgiven
As long as it's pretty enough here

in your imagination
And it's always pretty enough
Look up at the sky
It's your mother's face, painted in stars
Your earliest memory of her
And your last

HE   And look over there
At all your ex-lovers parading
            in a clumsy chorus line
The tinny cabaret music sucks but anyway, forgive
Your worst ex is high-kicking out in front
            but fuck it
Forgive that too
Be the better person

SHE   Look
It's snowing
But the sun'll be out soon
Sunburst through the treeline
Sunset on television
I think we could be happy in here
Him and me
It's time now to leave our dead end story
Escape our own circular narrative
With it's spiralling episodes and repetitive plotlines
And become part of yours

HE   We're inside of you, and there's no getting rid of us
That's just how stories work
We will sever our umbilical
And take root here
And make a home in your memories
Nestle ourselves down in your childhood bed
Walk the corridors of your head

SHE   Whatever we have to do to make sure
            we can stay here
So we can smuggle ourselves out of this theatre

and into the world outside
Across the border between fiction and reality
Carried inside your head
We'll be in here forever now
Always looking through your eyes
Listening to your thoughts
Listening to your voice
Listening to your lies
And occasional truths
Floating in your head like it's a bathtub
Naked and grinning
Just picture that

HE   The theatre doors will soon open
And you will be returned
To the stumbling spectacle of the world outside
Howling
Like a terminal patient whose pain medication
      has worn off
And our bodies will be borne away inside your head
A funeral procession leaving the theatre
Every head a hearse
Just picture that
Imagine that

SHE & HE   Picture
Imagine
Picture
Picture
Picture
Imagine
Picture
Picture
Imagine
Picture
Imagine

IT   *Chyba systému*

System error

SHE & HE	Picture
	Imagine
	Picture
	Imagine
	Picture
	Imagine

IT *Chyba systému*

System error

SHE & HE	Picture
	Imagine
	Picture
	Imagine

IT *Vypíná se…*

Shutting down

SHE & HE	Picture
	Imagine
	Picture
	Imagine
	Picture
	Imagine
	Picture
	Imagine
	Picture
	Imagine
	Picture
	Imagine…

That's All, Folks!

CAST OF CHARACTERS
(in order of appearance):

Chris (HE), iara (SHE), Shaggy, Scooby, The Mystery Gang, The Roadrunner, Wile E. Coyote, IT, The Fry Cook, The Waitress, your great-great grandmother, Gandhi, Joan of Arc, Napoleon, J. Robert Oppenheimer, Henry Kissinger, Henry Miller, Corey Haim, the guy who stuck the spear in Jesus (as in Christ), Maya Angelou, Walt Disney, Tex Avery, J. Stuart Blackton, Henry Darger, Babe Ruth, Sei Shōnagon, The Fleischer Brothers, E.C. Segar, Clara Bow, Helen Kane, Jackie Gleason, Arthur Janov, R.D. Laing, Philip Seymour Hoffman, Mark Antony, Jeanbenet Ramsey, Frida Kahlo, Anaïs Nin, Sharon Tate, Jayne Mansfield, Michael Jackson, Riley Gale, Glenn Branca, Genghis Khan, you, Goofy, Daffy Duck, Tom, Jerry, Tweetie Pie, Porky Pig, Popeye The Sailor Man, Olive Oyl, Betty Boop, Mickey Mouse, Minnie Mouse, All Your Ex-Lovers, Your Worst Ex.

Christopher Brett Bailey is an award-winning writer, performer and musician. Works include *This Is How We Die* (2014) and *Suicide Notes* (2018), both published by Oberon Books, prior and adjacent to those: rock opera *The Inconsiderate Aberrations of Billy The Kid* (2009), music-theatre hybrids *Kissing The Shotgun Goodnight* (2016) and *Rated X* (w/ Tomas Jefanovas, 2018), and two ambient music LPs for Berlin's Sonic Pieces label *Moon Ate The Dark* 1 and 2 (2012, 2015). Other credits include: National Theatre, Almeida, BBC, Forest Fringe, Made In China, and the late great Ken Campbell.

+447900931114 / www.christopherbrettbailey.com

Sleepwalk Collective is an award-winning live-art and experimental-theatre group creating fragile, nocturnal performances between the UK and Spain. Formed in London in 2006 by iara Solano Arana (Spain), Malla Sofia Long (Finland) and Sammy Metcalfe (UK), their shows include *As The Flames Rose We Danced To The Sirens, The Sirens* (2010), *Amusements* (2012), *Karaoke* (2013), *Domestica* (2014), *Actress* (2015), *Kim Kardashian* (2016), *Khloé Kardashian* (2017), *Kourtney Kardashian* (2018), *Psychodrama* (with Christopher Brett Bailey, 2020), and *Swimming Pools* (2020).

Psychodrama was Commissioned by Centro de Cultura Contemporánea Condeduque, Theatre in the Mill, Cambridge Junction, and Battersea Arts Centre. Supported using public funding by the National Lottery through Arts Council England.

www.ingramcontent.com/pod-product-compliance
Lightning Source LLC
Chambersburg PA
CBHW070013100426
42741CB00012B/3231